INVESTIGATING NATURAL DISASTERS

INVESTIGATING
HURRICANES

BY ELIZABETH ELKINS

raintree

a Capstone company — publishers for children

Raintree is an imprint of Capstone Global Library Limited, a company incorporated in England and Wales having its registered office at 264 Banbury Road, Oxford, OX2 7DY – Registered company number: 6695582

www.raintree.co.uk
myorders@raintree.co.uk

Edited by Alesha Sullivan
Designed by Steve Mead
Picture research by Morgan Walters
Production by Laura Manthe
Printed and bound in China.

ISBN 978 1 4747 3514 8
21 20 19 18 17
10 9 8 7 6 5 4 3 2 1

British Library Cataloguing in Publication Data
A full catalogue record for this book is available from the British Library.

Photo Credits
Alamy: RGB Ventures / SuperStock, 8; Getty Images: Joe Raedle, 16, 27; Newscom: CHINE NOUVELLE/SIPA, 15, MARICE COHN BAND/KRT, 21; Science Source: Spencer Sutton, 9; Shutterstock: CEW, 11, Coprid, middle 29, holbox, 12, 13, Leonard Zhukovsky, 18, 19, Marafona, Cover, Marc Pagani Photography, 22, Martin Good, 14, Nik Merkulov, (grunge texture) design element throughout, cover, Petr Malyshev, top 29, Prentiss, 4, tale, bottom 29, VladimirCeresnak, cover, design element throughout, wandee007, 7; Wikimedia: Walter Hellebrand, 24, 25

Every effort has been made to contact copyright holders of material reproduced in this book. Any omissions will be rectified in subsequent printings if notice is given to the publisher.

All the internet addresses (URLs) given in this book were valid at the time of going to press. However, due to the dynamic nature of the internet, some addresses may have changed, or sites may have changed or ceased to exist since publication. While the author and publisher regret any inconvenience this may cause readers, no responsibility for any such changes can be accepted by either the author or the publisher.

CONTENTS

LOST AT SEA

Wind gusts shook the aircraft. Giant waves and sea spray made it hard to see anything. But the National Oceanic and Atmospheric Administration (NOAA) Hurricane Hunters aeroplane kept flying. The plane dipped closer to the ocean's surface than normal. It was 2 October 2015, and Hurricane Joaquin was pounding the Bahamas. And the SS *El Faro*, a United States cargo ship, was missing in the storm.

Hurricane Joaquin brought huge amounts of rainfall and caused extensive damage along the US east coast.

HURRICANE CATEGORIES

Scientists have a system for ranking the strength of hurricanes. They are classified according to their wind speed. A Category 1 storm has the lightest winds and causes minor damage. A Category 3 storm can uproot some trees and damage small buildings. But a Category 5 storm, with winds greater than 250 kilometres (155 miles) per hour, can cause extreme damage or destruction. A Category 5 uproots trees, takes the roofs off houses and overturns vehicles.

Joaquin was a Category 5 hurricane. The storm moved across the Atlantic Ocean carrying heavy rains and flooding the southern US. Joaquin moved across the islands of the Bahamas, causing a large amount of damage. Then the hurricane swept near the island of Bermuda. Forecasters were afraid Joaquin would impact the United Kingdom, but the storm lost strength before it reached the area.

The SS *El Faro* was never found. The US Coast Guard located one body that they believed came from the ship and **debris**, including a life jacket and a deck chair. All 33 crew members died.

debris scattered pieces of something that has been destroyed or broken

RECIPE FOR A HURRICANE

A hurricane is a huge storm with high winds. They can last as long as a week, moving across the ocean. Many hurricanes form over warm ocean waters near the **equator**. But what are the ingredients needed to make a hurricane?

For a hurricane to grow, the storm must be at least 483 kilometres (300 miles) from the equator. Earth's movement causes the storm to begin spinning. Hurricanes also need certain weather conditions to develop, such as warm, moist air. This air must be at least 27 degrees Celsius (80 degrees Fahrenheit). As the warm air pushes upwards from the water, it leaves behind a low-pressure area close to the water's surface. More warm, moist air pushes into the low-pressure area and moves upwards. There, the air cools and **condenses** into water droplets. The warm air moving into the sky creates clouds and thunderstorms.

The thunderstorms gather and spin around a centre of low pressure. As the growing storm feeds on more warm water droplets **evaporating** from the ocean surface, the clouds rotate faster and faster until they become a hurricane. Most hurricanes lose energy and weaken when they hit land. They no longer have the warm water and air to keep them going.

Hurricanes first form over warm ocean waters.

FACT

Hurricanes, cyclones and typhoons are all words to describe the same kind of storm. It just depends on where they occur. They are called hurricanes in the Atlantic and northeast Pacific oceans. In the northwest Pacific, they are called typhoons. And in the South Pacific and Indian oceans, they are cyclones.

equator imaginary line around the middle of Earth, separating the northern and southern hemispheres

condense change from gas to liquid; water vapour condenses into liquid water

evaporate change from a liquid into a vapour or a gas

Hurricane Elena, as seen from space in 1985, slammed into the United States Gulf Coast.

A hurricane isn't a solid mass of swirling winds and clouds. At the very centre of a hurricane, there is a clear, calm area called the eye. The eye is about 32 to 64 kilometres (20 to 40 miles) across. The eye is a low-pressure area. While the warm, moist air is swirling around the eye, cool, dry air sinks into the eye from the sky above the storm. The cool air enters in-between the bands of clouds that surround the eye, which are called the eyewall. An aeroplane flying through a hurricane will pass through the eye and suddenly experience lighter winds and even blue skies above them. But then the plane will pass through the eyewall and back into the storm.

In coastal areas hurricanes cause storm surges. A storm surge is abnormally high water created by a storm. In a storm surge, the water level is higher than the normal level of the tide. A storm surge can cause flooding, especially if it happens at the same time as the usual high tide. Storm surges can be the most dangerous part of a hurricane.

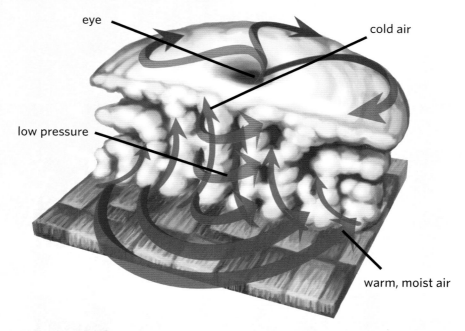

eye

cold air

low pressure

warm, moist air

FACT

A hurricane in Australia in 1899 set a storm surge record. The water was more than 12 metres (40 feet) high. The water was so high that fish and dolphins were later found on top of cliffs.

Climate change

The year 2015 was a record year for the greatest number of Category 4 and 5 hurricanes. This has made many people wonder if climate change is affecting hurricanes. Hurricanes are becoming stronger and are lasting longer. This is because hurricanes feed on the warm, moist ocean waters near the equator. Climate change is increasing the temperature of the world's oceans. This raises the temperatures on the surface of the water, where hurricanes gather their energy. It also means that hurricanes are gathering more moisture, resulting in record rainfalls.

Stronger hurricanes also cause more damage. Because the ocean water levels are rising, it takes less of a storm surge to flood coastal areas. And with the destruction of wetlands such as swamps, there are fewer areas that can hold excess water from hurricanes and large tropical storms. This means that more flooding can take place at a quicker pace.

FACT

Climate change, also called global warming, is a long-term change in the Earth's climate. Climate change is caused by an increased amount of **carbon dioxide** in the air due to burning fossil fuels for energy.

carbon dioxide colourless, odourless gas that people and animals breathe out

Areas of low ground near the coast are likely to flood during a hurricane or tropical storm.

DANGER ZONES

Some areas of the world are more likely to have hurricanes than others. Hurricanes form in the Atlantic Ocean, Gulf of Mexico and Caribbean Sea. They also form in the northeastern part of the Pacific Ocean. Hurricanes have a tendency to travel in a west-north-west direction, so they can hit the Atlantic coast off the United States or the Gulf of Mexico. Hurricanes also need warm ocean water to stay strong. The water off the Pacific coast of the US does not get warm enough to support hurricanes. The winds there also tend to drive storms away from the California coast.

Anyone living in a coastal region, including the US Atlantic coast, the Hawaiian Islands, and on Caribbean islands, can experience hurricanes. Low-lying US cities such as New Orleans, Louisiana, Virginia Beach, Virginia and Tampa, Florida, are at risk because the cities are close to sea level and can easily flood. Even cities further inland can be greatly affected by a hurricane's powerful winds and heavy rains.

Homes located on Caribbean islands were demolished during a hurricane disaster.

Hurricane season

Most hurricanes develop during a period known as hurricane season. In the eastern Pacific Ocean, hurricane season is from 15 May to 30 November. In the western Pacific and Indian oceans, it is from early January to late March. And in the Atlantic region, this period lasts from 1 June until 30 November. More than 95 per cent of major hurricanes occur during these months.

The most active time for hurricanes in the Atlantic Ocean is between August and mid-October. At this time of year, the water is warmest. The weather offers more heat energy to power storms to hurricane strength.

Secretary-General of the World Meteorological Organization Michel Jarraud presented information at a press conference regarding the world's increasing surface temperature, which could affect hurricane season worldwide.

The World Meteorological Organization is located in Geneva, Switzerland.

WORLD METEOROLOGICAL ORGANIZATION
ORGANISATION METEOROLOGIQUE MONDIALE

What's in a name?

Why are hurricanes given names? Naming the storm makes it easier to avoid confusion for **forecasters**, especially if two storms happen at the same time. Forecasters started naming storms in 1953, and until 1979, the storms were only given female names.

Since 1979, both male and female names are used in turn in alphabetical order. The World Meteorological Organization (WMO) puts together the storm name list. The names of extremely destructive hurricanes are retired. This is done out of respect for people who were hurt or killed by the storm. The WMO decides when a name is retired.

forecaster someone who calculates or predicts weather conditions

Predicting a hurricane

Predicting a hurricane's path can be difficult. The winds that push these storms along the coast can be irregular. But forecasters use certain tools to give people an idea of the hurricane's path, how strong the storm will be and who will be affected. Forecasters watch tropical storms developing by using **satellite** images. These images can show wind speed, clouds and temperature.

A meteorologist in Miami, Florida, USA, looks at a computer model tracking Hurricane Isabel in 2003.

JOSEPH B. DUCKWORTH

On 27 July 1943, off the coast of Texas, USA, Colonel Joseph B. Duckworth was the first person to safely fly through a hurricane. Duckworth was enlisted in the US Air Force. He had many years of experience with instrument flights. Instruments such as electronic signals control instrument flights. Pilots must fly using instruments when the weather conditions are not safe and they can't rely on visual navigation.

Crews in aeroplanes also use weather instruments to gather data. Imagine flying into a hurricane's dark clouds. Special planes called Hurricane Hunters fly directly into hurricanes. The aircrew collects data on wind direction and speed, air pressure and temperature. The crew then sends this data back to scientists at the National Hurricane Centre in Miami, Florida, USA. The information collected helps experts learn how fast the storm is moving and where it is headed. If necessary, forecasters issue watches and warnings to the public. These warnings tell people to get ready for a storm or to **evacuate** their homes.

satellite spacecraft that circles Earth; satellites gather and send information

evacuate leave an area during a time of danger

THE AFTERMATH

After a hurricane, many people's lives are uprooted. Floods may make roads impossible to drive on. Damaged bridges could collapse under the weight of a car. Houses may be without roofs. Entire buildings can be reduced to rubble. Even people whose homes survived the storm may be without power for days or even weeks. Sometimes food can be unsafe to eat, and water can be unsafe to drink.

In areas hit by hurricanes, people must rebuild homes, businesses and roads destroyed by the storm. Often people will rebuild homes higher off the ground to help prevent future flooding or damage. Roads and bridges are built better and stronger.

Hurricanes also damage the environment. Winds rip off tree limbs, and islands disappear under water. Waves can tear away at the shoreline, carrying away chunks of land. Eventually the environment begins to recover, but it may show the scars of a hurricane for years to come.

FACT

When a hurricane strikes the US, the American Red Cross is ready. This group helps people in emergencies. The Red Cross sets up shelters to house people during the storm. They also provide clothing, food and medicine when necessary.

After a hurricane near Long Beach, New York, USA, homes along the beachfront were completely wrecked.

THE WORLD'S WORST HURRICANES

Many places in the world have experienced terrible, damaging hurricanes. On 3 September 1988, Hurricane Gilbert struck Jamaica. It was the most destructive storm in the island's history. It was a Category 3 storm with winds more than 240 kilometres (150 miles) per hour. The storm spent an entire day moving across the island. Almost 76 centimetres (30 inches) of rain fell. There was a 2.5-metre (9-foot) storm surge, resulting in severe **flash flooding**. Three people died, and there was billions of pounds worth of damage.

FACT

Because of Hurricane Gilbert's high winds, the trees in the jungle on the Yucatan Peninsula lost nearly all their leaves. The forest lost 30 per cent of its trees.

flash flood sudden and destructive rush of water down a narrow gully or over a sloping surface, caused by heavy rainfall

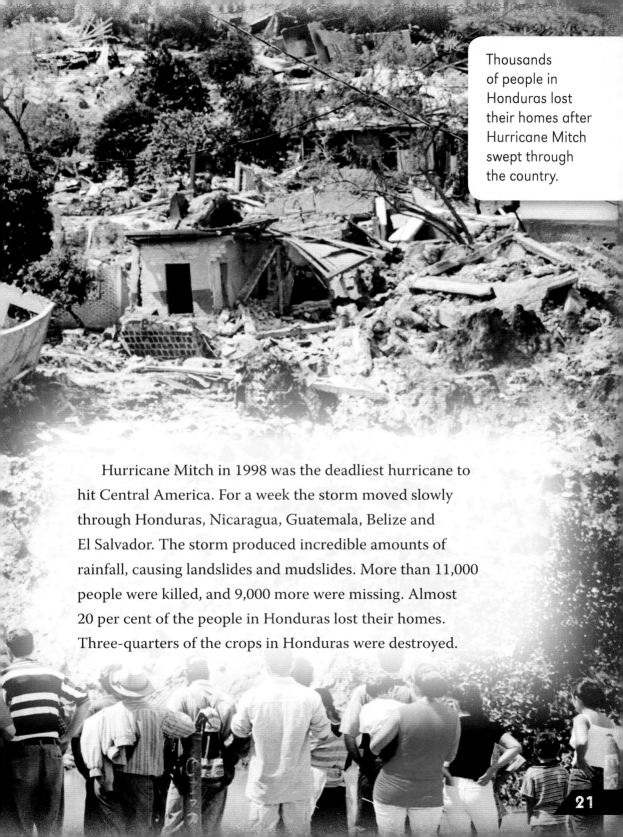

Thousands of people in Honduras lost their homes after Hurricane Mitch swept through the country.

Hurricane Mitch in 1998 was the deadliest hurricane to hit Central America. For a week the storm moved slowly through Honduras, Nicaragua, Guatemala, Belize and El Salvador. The storm produced incredible amounts of rainfall, causing landslides and mudslides. More than 11,000 people were killed, and 9,000 more were missing. Almost 20 per cent of the people in Honduras lost their homes. Three-quarters of the crops in Honduras were destroyed.

Hurricane Katrina left behind the most damage in New Orleans, Louisiana, USA.

The east coast of the United States sees many strong hurricanes with an average of two every year. One of the worst hurricanes to reach the United States was Hurricane Katrina in 2005. Katrina hit New Orleans, Louisiana. The storm was 645 kilometres (400 miles) across and had wind speeds of 225 kilometres (140 miles) per hour. The **levees** that protected the city from Lake Pontchartrain broke. The storm surge flooded New Orleans until 80 per cent of the city was under water. People had to be evacuated, and many drowned. The storm killed 2,000 people. Katrina caused more than £75 billion in damages, making this storm the most expensive natural disaster in US history.

The hurricane that hit Galveston, Texas, in 1900 was even worse. It killed between 8,000 and 12,000 people. The storm flooded the city with a 4.5-metre (15-foot) storm surge. Even though people were warned to evacuate the city before the storm, many did not. Much of the city was destroyed. This hurricane is considered to be the worst weather-related disaster in US history in terms of the number of people killed.

levee bank built up near a river to prevent flooding

Flooding is expected to happen more frequently in the future because of climate change. The amount of rain that falls during the heaviest downpours is increasing as the average temperature is increasing in some regions. This is because warmer air holds more moisture than colder air. If the temperatures around the world continue to increase, scientists predict that rainfall may also increase by as much as 40 per cent. More rainfall will mean more flooding. Higher sea levels will also bring more flooding to coastal areas.

THE COSTLIEST HURRICANES

Hurricanes can be very expensive. They rip apart buildings and send trees and power line poles crashing down. Roads become covered with floodwater and blocked by debris. Businesses are destroyed. Homes are battered by winds and soaked by rain. Families can lose everything.

KATRINA

2005
Category 3
£83 billion

Humans often make choices that increase the chances of their homes flooding. People are building homes and other structures on floodplains, so when rivers rise, the chances of flooding are greater. People are also paving over more of the landscape for roads and car parks. Paved surfaces do not absorb water. When there is a heavy downpour, the water has to flow to unpaved areas, which can cause flooding.

FACT

The word *hurricane* comes from the name of an ancient Mayan storm god, Hunraken. The Taino people of the Caribbean also had an evil god named Huracan.

SANDY

2012
Category **1**
£38 billion

IKE

2008
Category **2**
£22.5 billion

ANDREW

1992
Category **5**
£20 billion

WILMA

2005
Category **3**
£16 billion

PLANNING FOR DISASTER

Scientists and weather researchers continue to look for ways to better forecast the path and intensity of developing hurricanes. They study data from past hurricanes and look for patterns that will help them better understand how these storms form, grow and then fall apart. They use computer models to help them forecast how hurricanes may develop and move. They are also studying the potential effects of climate change on hurricanes.

PREVENTATIVE MEASURES

Some engineering practices can help prevent floods from getting out of control. Car parks paved with a special type of concrete that water can seep through are less likely to flood. Rain gardens are dips in the land, planted with shrubs, flowers and bushes. When water fills the dip, it holds the water as the plants soak up the excess through their roots. A balancing lake, also called a flood pond, is a dry area meant to contain extra water during a storm. These ponds are usually located next to rivers, streams and lakes.

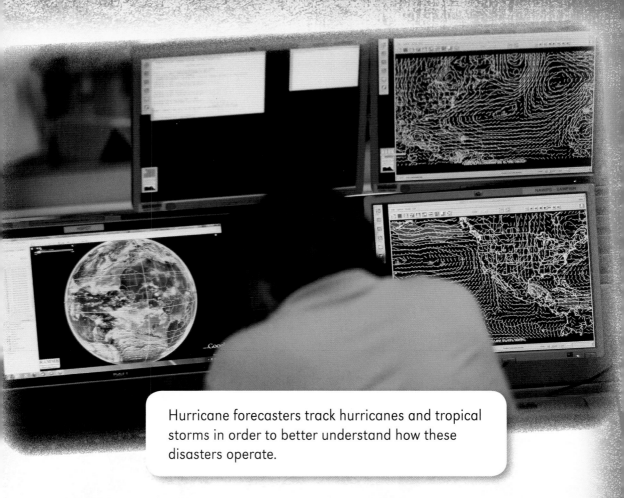

Hurricane forecasters track hurricanes and tropical storms in order to better understand how these disasters operate.

Architects and **engineers** are designing buildings that can better withstand hurricanes. This includes ways to anchor roofs to walls so that they are less likely to fly off. It also means tying mobile homes down to their foundations, so they won't be lifted by strong winds. Windows can be constructed with plastic or with protective glass coatings so that they are less likely to shatter. And any home can add hurricane shutters, which quickly and easily cover doors and windows to protect them.

engineer someone trained to design and build machines, vehicles, bridges, roads and other structures

STAYING SAFE

For people who live in areas where hurricanes occur, it is important to know how to stay safe. They must listen to weather forecasts and be ready to evacuate their home if they are told to do so.

As part of general hurricane preparedness, homeowners should trim any large trees around their homes, have plywood ready to cover doors and windows and put away any loose garden items. Families should have a hurricane plan so that everyone knowns what to do and where to go during a storm.

People should never remain in their homes if they have been ordered to evacuate. But if they are told to stay, they should keep away from windows and doors, find an interior room on the first floor, and get under a table or other sturdy object. When an evacuation is recommended, it is also important to have a storm kit ready to take with you to shelter or a safe place. Your emergency kit should include items you may need for a few days.

AN EMERGENCY KIT SHOULD HAVE:

- **first aid kit**

- **bottled water**

- **prescription medicines**

- **baby food and nappies**

- **cards, games and books**

- **toiletries**

- **battery-powered radio**

- **torch (one per person)**

- **extra batteries**

- **blankets or sleeping bags**

- **identification**

- **valuable papers (insurance)**

- **credit card or cash**

FIRST AID KIT

GLOSSARY

carbon dioxide colourless, odourless gas that people and animals breathe out

condense change from gas to liquid; water vapour condenses into liquid water

debris scattered pieces of something that has been destroyed or broken

engineer someone trained to design and build machines, vehicles, bridges, roads and other structures

equator imaginary line around the middle of Earth, separating the northern and southern hemispheres

evacuate leave an area during a time of danger

evaporate change from a liquid into a vapour or a gas

flash flood sudden and destructive rush of water down a narrow gully or over a sloping surface, caused by heavy rainfall

forecaster someone who calculates or predicts weather conditions

levee bank built up near a river to prevent flooding

satellite spacecraft that circles Earth; satellites gather and send information

READ MORE

Hurricanes (Nature Unleashed), Louise Spilsbury and Richard Spilsbury (Franklin Watts, 2017)

Superstorms (Planet in Peril), Cath Senker (Wayland, 2014)

Surviving Hurricanes (Children's True Stories), Elizabeth Raum and HL Studios (Raintree, 2012)

WEBSITES

www.bbc.co.uk/newsround/34615665
Find out how storm categories are decided and what they mean.

**news.bbc.co.uk/cbbcnews/hi/newsid_2290000/
newsid_2296600/2296669.stm**
Find out all about hurricanes, typhoons and cyclones, including animated guides.

www.ngkids.co.uk/science-and-nature/Hurricanes
Discover amazing facts and figures about hurricanes on the National Geographic children's website.

COMPREHENSION QUESTIONS

1. Why do hurricanes form in ocean waters by the equator? Why don't they form in northern waters?

2. Why do forecasters use many different tools – such as aeroplanes, ships and computers – to track hurricanes?

3. Why do scientists think climate change might affect hurricanes, and how?

INDEX